EASY PIECES FOR ACOUSTIC GUITAR

T0056436

WISE PUBLICATIONS
part of The Music Sales Group
London/New York/Paris/Sydney/Copenhagen/Berlin/Madrid/Tokyo

Published by
Wise Publications
14-15 Berners Street, London W1T 3LJ, UK.

Exclusive Distributors:
Music Sales Limited
Distribution Centre, Newmarket Road, Bury St Edmunds, Suffolk IP33 3YB, UK.
Music Sales Pty Limited
20 Resolution Drive, Caringbah, NSW 2229, Australia.

Order No. AM995555
ISBN: 978-1-84772-751-0
This book © Copyright 2009 Wise Publications,
a division of Music Sales Limited.

Music arranged by Mark Currey.
Edited by Rachel Payne.
Guitar demonstrations on CD by Mark Currey.
CD recorded, mixed and mastered by Jonas Persson.

Printed in the EU.

Your Guarantee of Quality
As publishers, we strive to produce every book to the highest commercial standards.
This book has been carefully designed to minimise awkward page turns and to make playing from it a real pleasure.
Particular care has been given to specifying acid-free, neutral-sized paper made from
pulps which have not been elemental chlorine bleached.
This pulp is from farmed sustainable forests and was produced with special regard for the environment.
Throughout, the printing and binding have been planned to ensure a sturdy,
attractive publication which should give years of enjoyment.
If your copy fails to meet our high standards, please inform us and we will gladly replace it.

www.musicsales.com

ALL THROUGH THE NIGHT

Traditional

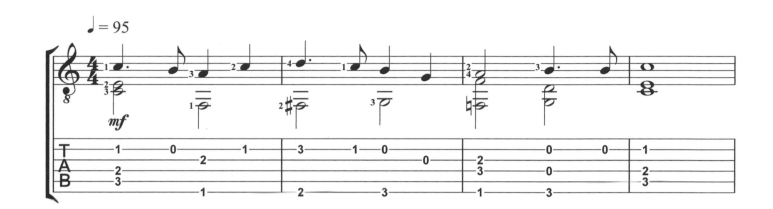

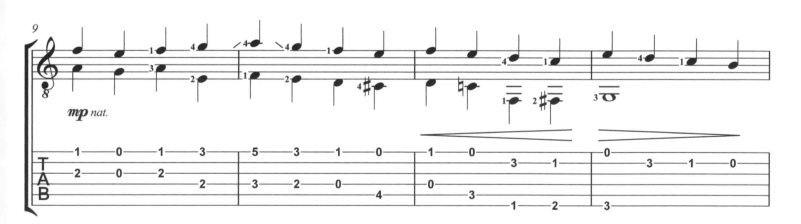

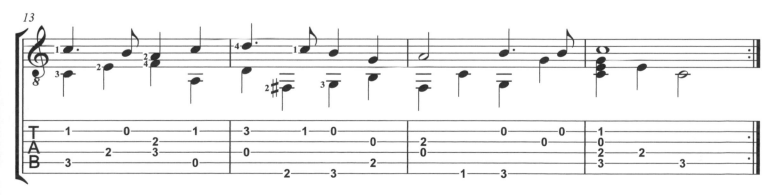

Amazing Grace

Words by John Newton
Traditional Music

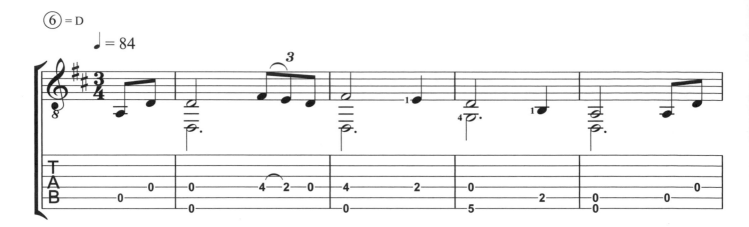

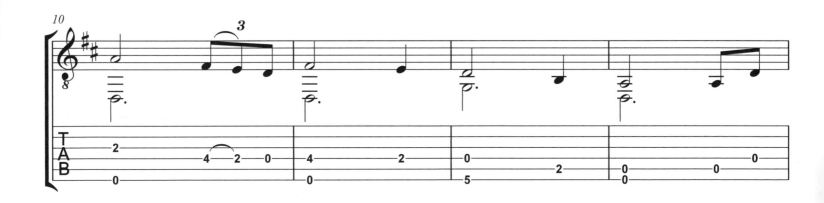

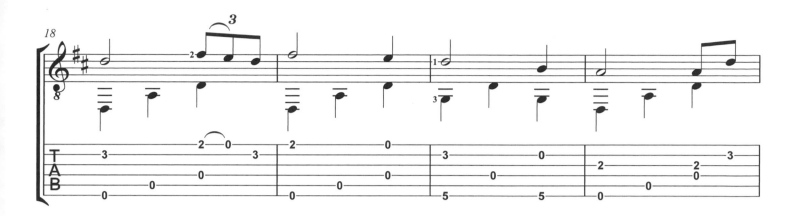

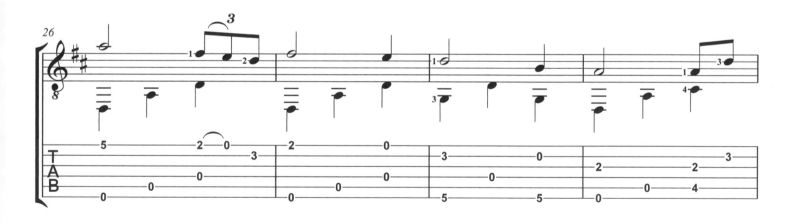

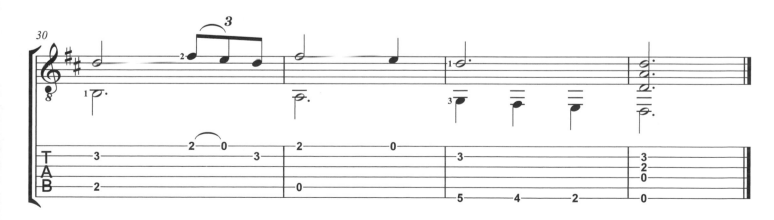

Auld Lang Syne

Words by Robert Burns
Traditional Music

♩ = 90

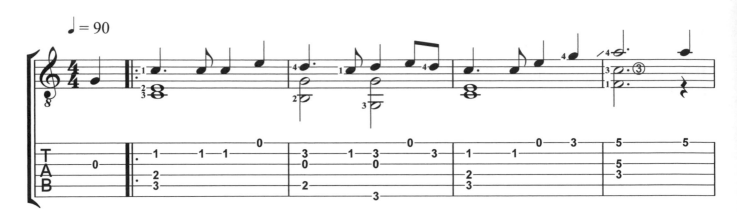

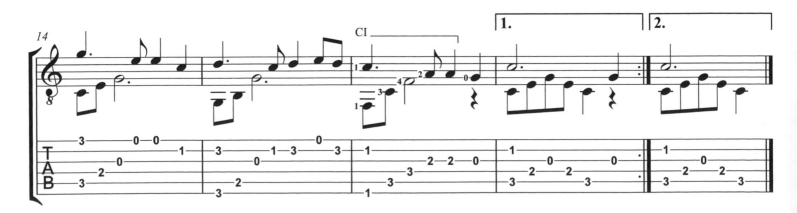

DAVID OF THE WHITE ROCK

Traditional

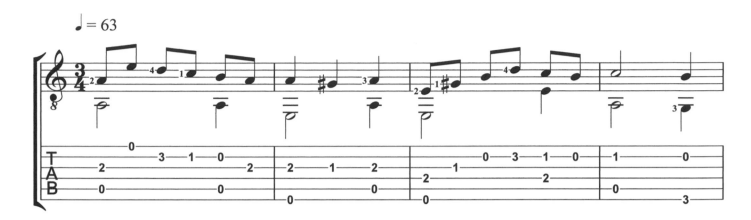

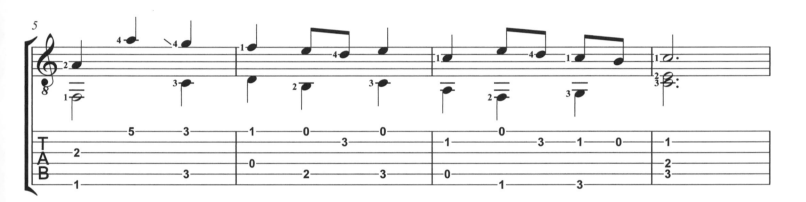

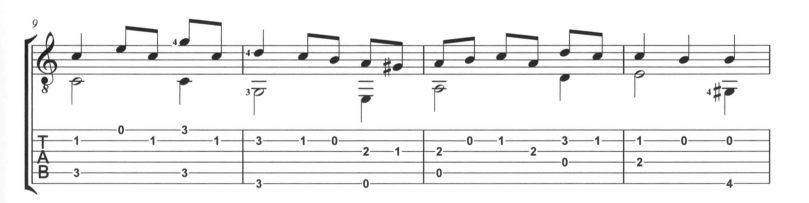

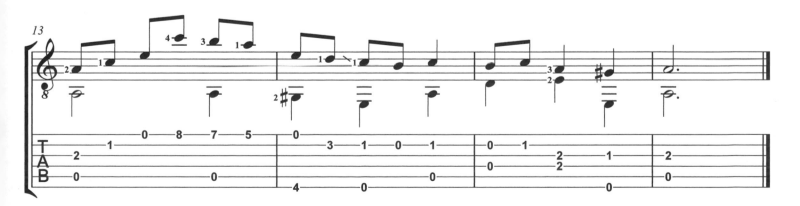

Canon in D

Composed by Johann Pachelbel

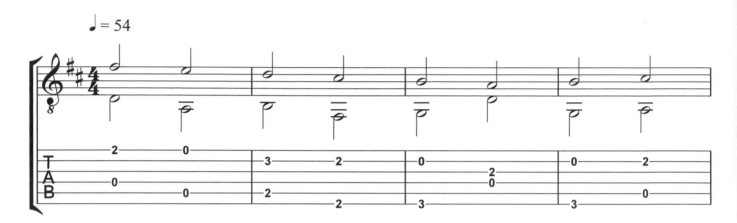

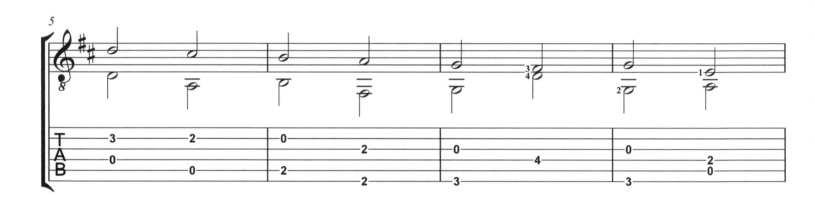

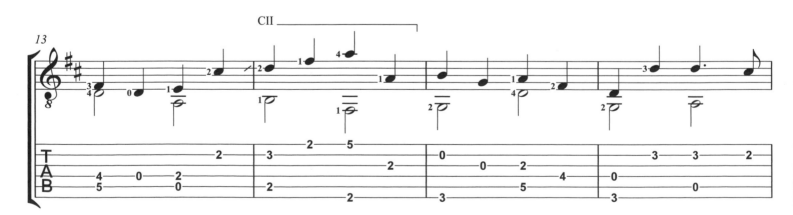

9

10

11

Danny Boy

Traditional Irish Melody

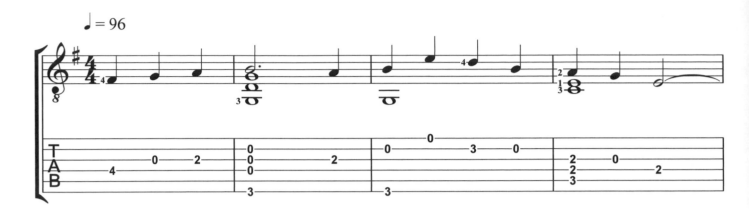

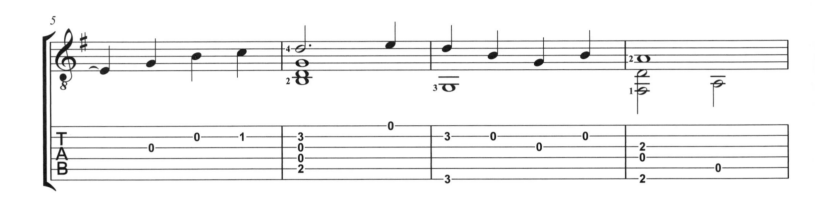

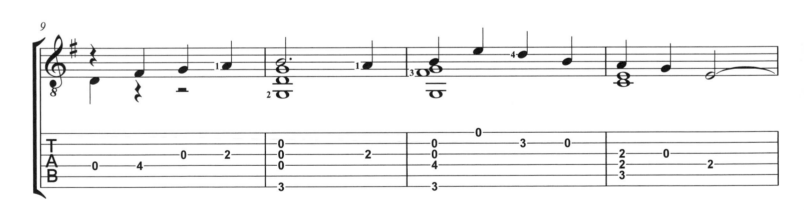

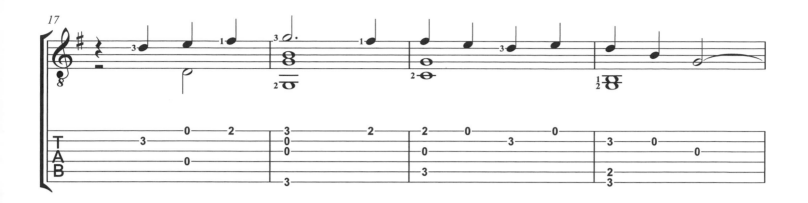

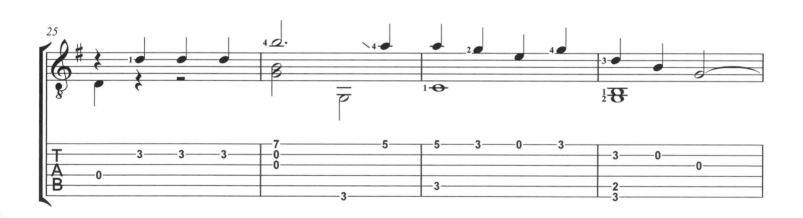

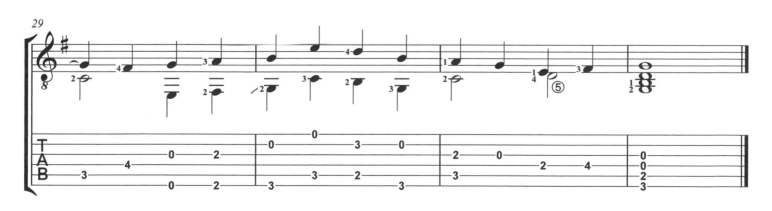

13

Greensleeves

Traditional

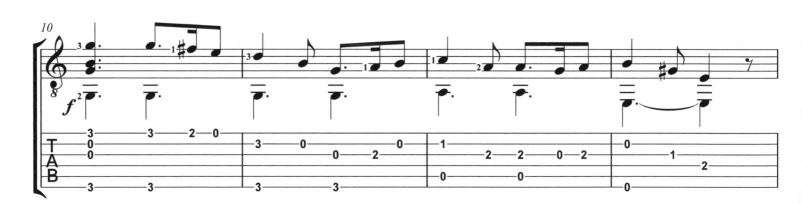

HABAÑERA
(from 'Carmen')

Composed by Georges Bizet

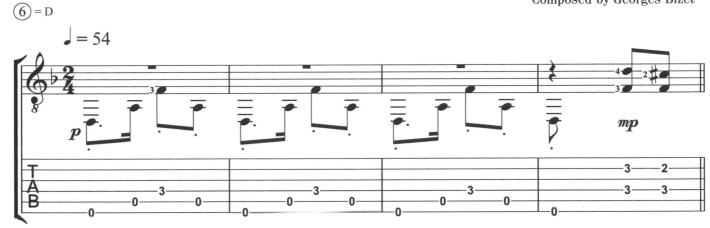

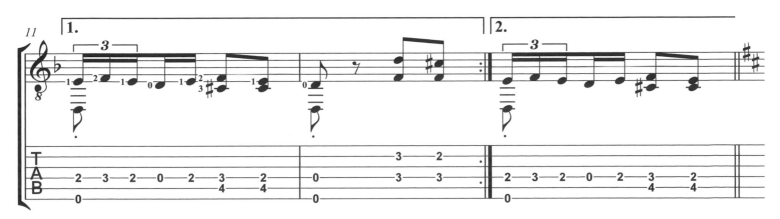

16

HOUSE OF THE RISING SUN

Traditional

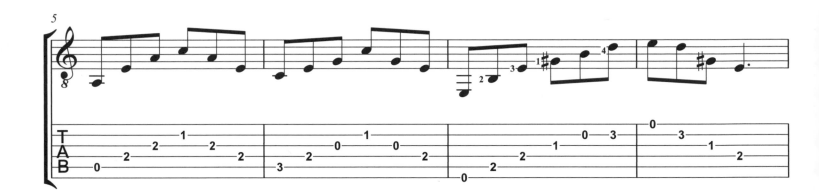

To Coda ⊕

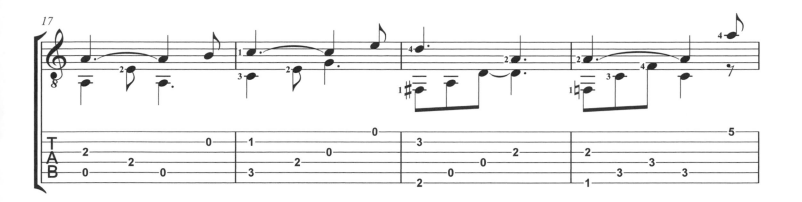

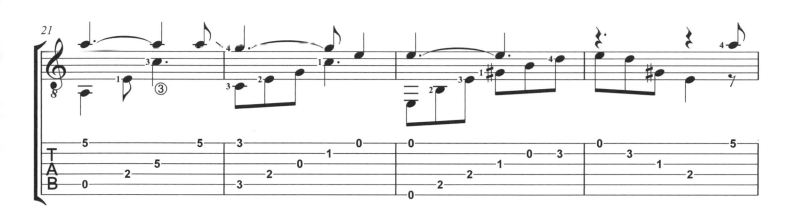

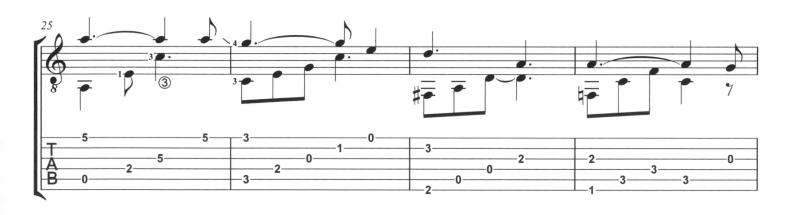

19

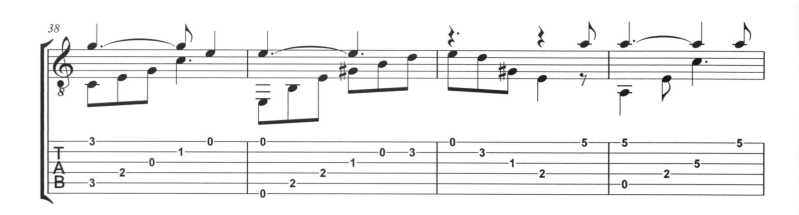

D.C. al Coda

⊕ *Coda*

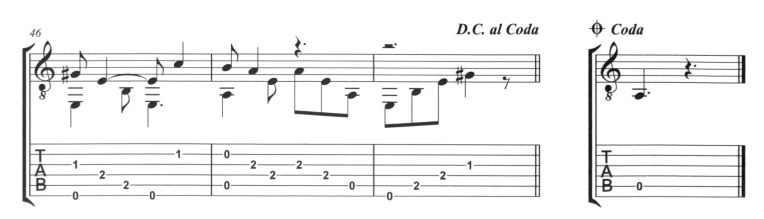

MINUET
(from 'Music For The Royal Fireworks')

Composed by George Frideric Handel

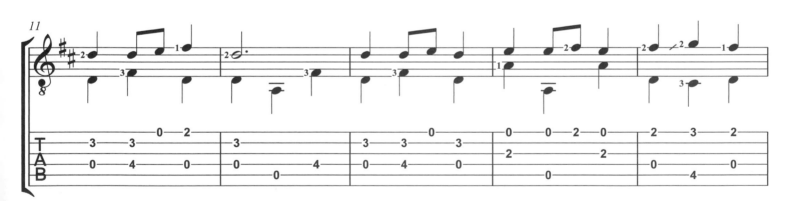

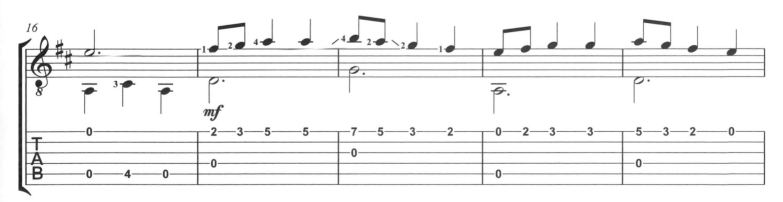

Scarborough Fair

Traditional

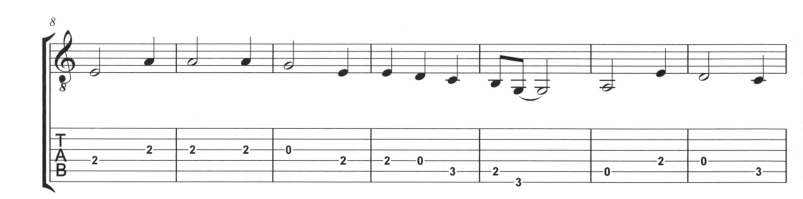

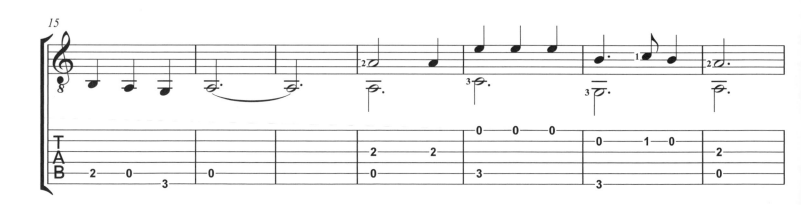

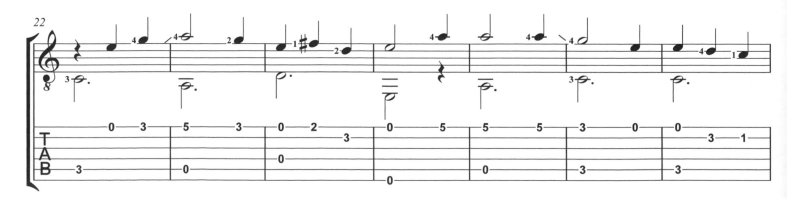

SKYE BOAT SONG

Traditional

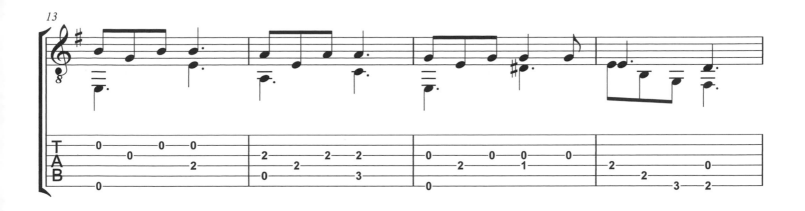

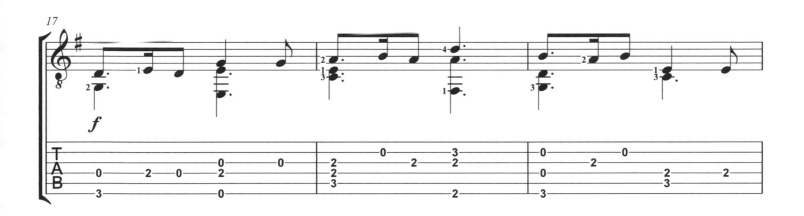

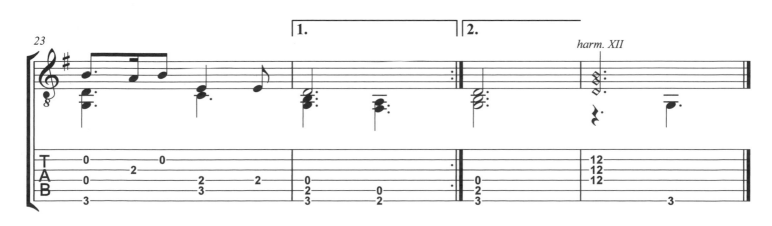

SPRING (FIRST MOVEMENT THEME)
from 'The Four Seasons'

Composed by Antonio Vivaldi

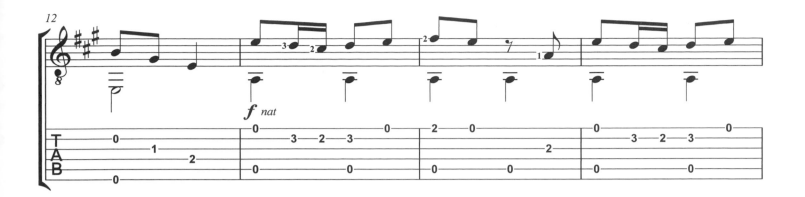

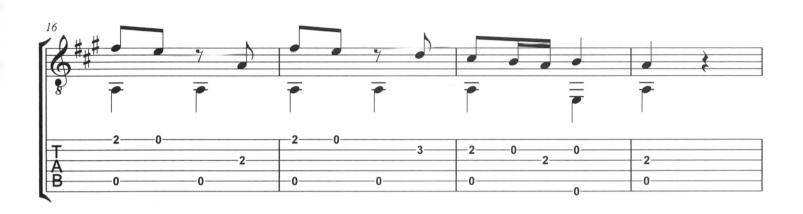

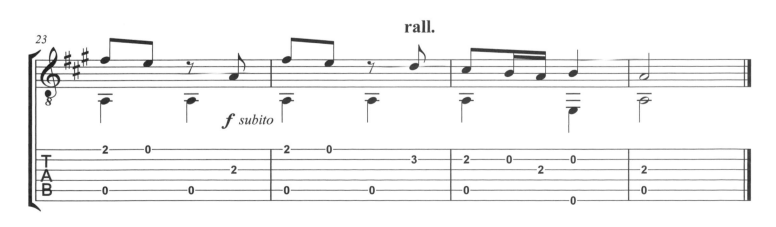

WADE IN THE WATER

Traditional

31

Silent Night

Words by Joseph Mohr
Music by Franz Gruber

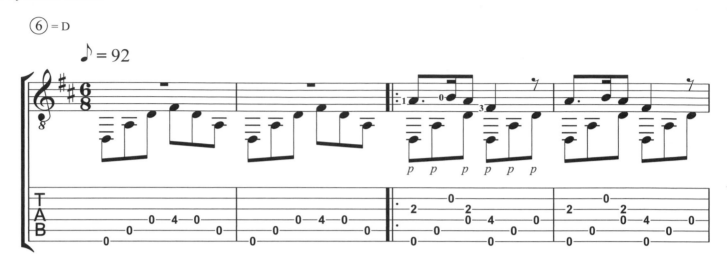

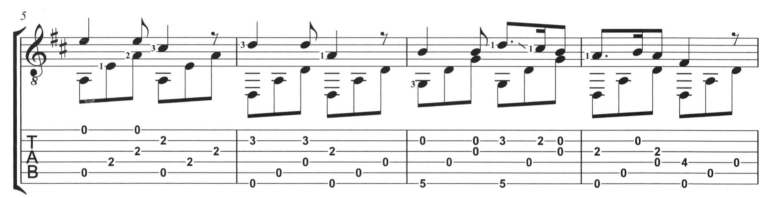

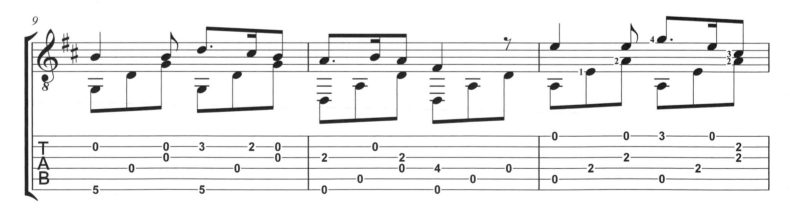

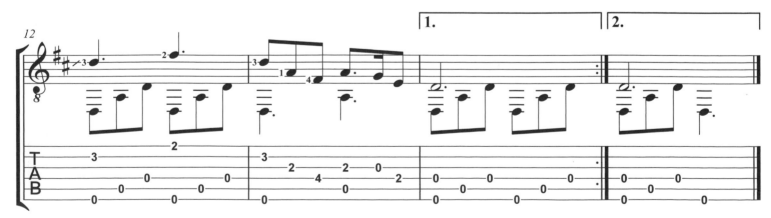

1 2 3 4 5 6 7 8 9